Robert Russell Booth, George Andrew Lewis

A memorial of Lieut

Franklin Butler Crosby, of the Fourth Regiment U. S. Artillery

Robert Russell Booth, George Andrew Lewis

A memorial of Lieut
Franklin Butler Crosby, of the Fourth Regiment U. S. Artillery

ISBN/EAN: 9783743322523

Manufactured in Europe, USA, Canada, Australia, Japa

Cover: Foto ©ninafisch / pixelio.de

Manufactured and distributed by brebook publishing software
(www.brebook.com)

Robert Russell Booth, George Andrew Lewis

A memorial of Lieut

A MEMORIAL

OF

Lieut. Franklin Butler Crosby,

OF THE FOURTH REGIMENT U. S. ARTILLERY,

WHO WAS KILLED AT CHANCELLORSVILLE, VA.,
MAY 3, 1863.

"Brief, brave, and glorious was his young career."

New-York:
ANSON D. F. RANDOLPH,
683 BROADWAY.
1864.

INTRODUCTION.

THE patriot's devotion to his country ranks only next to the Christian's devotion to his Lord; and when patriotic ardor is vitalized by Christian faith, it must impart a true heroic beauty to the character, which will render it illustrious in any sphere of life. We who in these days are paying so terrible a price for national existence have constant need to keep in mind the grand moral meaning of our struggle, and to realize the tone and spirit which animates our sons and brothers in their endurance unto death. Certainly, one of the marked features of our historic era is the readiness with which *the young men* of the loyal States

have comprehended its real import, and
the alacrity with which they have arisen
to meet the grand emergency.

While politicians wavered, and old
men trembled before the coming shock,
our heroic youth saw with clear intui-
tion the line of duty, and rising in
mighty multitudes, pledged the ardor
of their brave and loyal hearts to the
rescue and salvation of the country.

It is impossible for any candid mind
to mistake the spirit which has inspired
their voluntary sacrifices. An innate love
for military service has had as little to
do with it as the mere mercenary mo-
tive which, in other lands, often trans-
forms the citizen into the soldier, solely
that he may escape the ills of poverty.
The most favored sons of fortune, the
educated and refined, have accepted their
portion in this bloody baptism as cheer-
fully as those to whom hardship was

familiar, and life an uncertain and adventurous quest.

The explanation can be found only in the wholesome influence of our free institutions, and in that wide diffusion of Christian principle which has taught our youth that loyalty and truth and righteousness are always to be preferred to selfish ease and a material prosperity. Not useless to the nation in its time of sorest need have been the painful labors of the Church of Christ. Our Sabbaths sanctified, our Sunday-schools established far and wide, our glorious revivals sweeping across the land, with all the inspiration of a higher life, have been the means, under God, of lifting our generation to the heights of moral principle, on which alone the crisis could be met, and the struggle sustained, until its victorious consummation. A Christian heroism has been,

in a large degree, the main spring of this
mighty movement, and has called forth
these loyal bands to guard the liberties
their fathers won — knowing full well
the cost, and willing to pay it down in
rivers of blood, for the grand recom-
pense.

To recognize this unshrinking valor
in our youth, and to bless God for its
well-timed display, is the spontaneous
impulse of every loyal heart. To send
amid their shattered ranks the nation's
blessing, to minister to their mutilated
bodies, in camp and hospital, by the
sympathy and practical relief they need,
and to place over their lowly graves the
record of a gratitude that shall endure
while memory survives — this is the
duty which we owe them, in the precious interest of liberty — in the sacred
name of Christ.

Evidently, then, nothing can be more

fitting than to perpetuate, in a permanent expression, the moral lineaments and life-work of those who have fallen in this glorious service. We rejoice in those contributions to our "living literature," which have already made the lives of Frazer Stearns, Adjutant Bacon, Sergeant Thompson, and Chaplain Fuller a continuous power for lofty impulse and self-sacrifice among us.

The name inscribed on this memorial is a fit companion for the noblest of these martyrs for liberty and Union.

Circumstances which need not be here detailed have as yet prevented an elaborate and finished record of his life; but for the sake of a large circle of sorrowing friends — and it is also hoped for public interest and profit — the following pages have been put in print.

They consist chiefly of the addresses made at the funeral, in the Mercer street

Church, New-York, to which his remains had been brought for the last offices of religion, where, on the twentieth of May, a large congregation gathered to honor his precious memory.

Imperfectly as these published fragments can set forth the beauty and devotion of this young life, so courageously surrendered at the behest of duty, they may avail to add one more voice to the many witnesses who, from the churchyards and cemeteries of our land, proclaim the heroism of our young men, and the value of the institutions thus loyally defended to the death. Hallowing their memories, perpetuating their spirit, cherishing in our heart of hearts the cause they loved so well, let those who still survive think tenderly of those who made their lives the ransom for the State.   R. R. B.

ADDRESS

OF

REV. ROBERT R. BOOTH.

———•◆•———

IT is, my friends, a precious consolation for us to know, amid the ordinary troubles of our earthly lot, and more especially when the bitter sorrow which death brings befalls us, that "affliction cometh not forth from the dust, neither doth trouble spring out of the ground." "It is the Lord, let him do what seemeth good in his sight." "The Lord gave and the Lord hath taken away; blessed be the name of the Lord." "I was dumb; I opened not my mouth because thou didst it."

These were the utterances of God's afflicted servants, in the olden time; and in this recognition of a will that ought to be supreme, of a wisdom that can never err, and of a love that is personal, tender, and eternal, there is reason for comfort in the bitterest bereavements of our mortal life.

I well know that it is sometimes hard for us to realize that such blows can fall upon us from a loving hand. Certainly, if we look only at the present anguish and bereavement, if we think only of the hopes which have been blighted, of the sweet fel-lowship cut off, and the drear vacancy that now remains, we shall be cast down and desolate, as we cry in our anguish: "All thy waves and billows have gone over me." But I speak on God's authority, and from experience too, in saying that we must read these dark pages, in the book of Providence, by the light of God's revealed, eternal love, if we would catch their true meaning, and find our chastisement "joyous and not grievous."

Life is the sovereign gift of

God alone. He dates its rising, orders its progress, and ordains its moment of transition. It should always be remembered by us, in our times of loss, that while earthly friends have been longing and praying for its continuance, One mightier in wisdom and in love may have been interceding for a contrary result, according to his own precious word: "Father, I will that they also whom thou hast given me be *with me* where I am, that they may behold my glory."

" Say, mourner, wouldst thou have preferred that heard
Had been the prayer of earth or that of heaven;

Eternal bliss deferred or realized,
The cross continued, or the kingdom
      won ?"

Ours, my friends, is a time of
costly sacrifices, of widespread
desolations, of sorrows which fall
heavily on our once peaceful
homes.   Our country's service
is exacting now "the price of
blood." For liberty, and union,
and the supremacy of law, how
many thousands are wasting with
disease, or mutilated with gaping
wounds, or lying in the solemn
calm of death, like this dear
youth before us! Among these
many martyred patriots, not one
has fallen more worthy of our

sincere affection and grateful memory than he.

When a young man of such rare promise and true nobility of character has finished his course in the presence of the nation and for its defense, it is the duty and the privilege of those who feel that he died for them to proclaim his virtues, and impress the example of his beautiful career.

He whom we mourn to-day was, in a peculiar sense, the child of this church, having been brought here in his infancy to the baptismal font, and having grown up in vital union with all the ordinances and privileges of this house of God.

It is, therefore, the occasion of sincere thanksgiving that it has pleased God to permit us to receive his precious dust among us, and from this scene of his own Christian faith and labors, to bear it to the house appointed for all the living.

FRANKLIN BUTLER CROSBY was born on the fourth of February, 1841, being the first child of Mr. John P. and Mrs. Margaret Butler Crosby. His baptismal name was derived from his maternal grandfather, Benjamin Franklin Butler, between whom and this first-born of his

children's children there existed
the most tender and affectionate
sympathy, a tie of earthly love
now purified and made perpetual
in God's heavenly kingdom.

As a child of the covenant,
Frank was successively connect-
ed with the infant-class, the
Sabbath-school, and with the
church, to which, when under
the pastoral charge of the Rev.
Dr. Prentiss, he united on the
eighteenth of October, 1854, being at the time thirteen years of
age. Afterward he was connect-
ed with the young men's Bible-
class, and with the mission-school
in Avenue D, where he continued to labor as a faithful teacher

until his departure from the city. He was also interested and active in the young men's prayer-meeting. Thus, in the church of God, he lived and grew to manhood in relations which became continually closer to all that is lovely and of good report.

It would hardly be appropriate for me to speak, in a public assembly, of that domestic life in which the tenderness of his filial and fraternal love was blended with the graces of his growing manhood; making him so obedient, so helpful, so discreet, that those who were related to him thus lavished upon him the fullness of their hearts.

After his graduation at the Free Academy in 1860, he entered the law-office of his father, and gave diligent attention to his elected calling.

Soon after this, the flame of civil war was kindled in the land, and he immediately prepared to give a loyal and hearty support to his country's cause. His health was vigorous, his form a model of perfect manhood, and he numbered himself, from the beginning, among those who ought to go to the war.

At this time he joined a regiment then organizing in the city, to be prepared for active service when the country should require its aid.

After the battle of Bull Run, he felt that he was imperatively summoned to the field. A commission as Second Lieutenant in the Fourth Regiment, U. S. Artillery, was soon obtained, and he joined his regiment at Fort McHenry, in August, 1861.

He was soon promoted, for good conduct and ability, to be the First Lieutenant; and, on the appointment of Captain Best, his commanding officer, to the post of Chief of Artillery in the Twelfth Army Corps, Lieutenant Crosby became the acting commander of his company, an honorable and responsible position, whose arduous duties he ever performed to the entire satisfaction of his superiors. Of the various services which he rendered to the cause in this relation it would be impossible for me to speak as they deserve.

During the winter of 1861 and 1862 he was stationed with his battery in General Banks's division, which was then guarding the line of the Potomac, above the Monocacy. Here he saw constant service, and had a full share in all the labors of that arduous winter.

At one time prostrated by a severe attack of fever, on his

recovery stationed at Harper's Ferry, afterward with the advance down the valley of Virginia to Harrisonburgh; guarding the rear in Banks's retreat from Winchester, and bringing off all his guns in safety; ardent in action, courageous in reverses; always anxious for the most active service; careful of his men, unsparing of himself; courteous toward the population around him—he continually sustained the character of the patriot soldier and the Christian gentleman.

In a letter written from this locality, and received since his death, it is remarked : "He has

left a truly honorable name in
this community, and every one
who knew him here in his life-
time, now that he is dead, has
an expression of regret for his
untimely fall, and a word of
praise for his memory."

During the spring of the present year he was stationed with
his company at Stafford Court-
House, in Virginia, until he was
ordered to the front to partici-
pate in the recent movements
of the army. A letter which
he wrote in January will reveal
the spirit with which he stood
in his appointed lot. After de-
ploring the ill success which had
attended so many efforts, and

the failure to achieve decisive victories, he adds: "Each one, however, must do his duty, work out his own part of the great plan; and, although knowing and lamenting existing errors, which are beyond his control, must not be discouraged, but, with a pure intention and a firm trust in God, go forward on his path of duty."

It was in such a spirit that he marched with his men to join in the wild storm of battle which was soon to rage in the wilderness on the south bank of the Rappahannock.

On the second day of May, his battery was stationed at

Chancellorsville, and was active-
ly engaged, with some loss,
though he himself escaped all
harm. On the evening of that
day his guns were well posted,
in readiness for service, and sent
forth their volleys through the
night, assisting to repel the as-
sault of " Stonewall " Jackson.

Early on the morning of the
third, another attack was made
by the enemy upon a ridge,
where his battery, with several
others, about thirty guns in all,
had been massed to check their
furious charge. The onset was
bravely met, and the conflict
prolonged for hours about that
spot.. Many brave men there

yielded up their lives, and among
them it pleased God that Lieutenant Crosby should be numbered. At half-past eight, on
that fair Sabbath morning, a
bullet from a sharpshooter, who
had secretly gained the right
flank of the battery, and had sin-
gled out its commander, pierced
his breast, and in about five
minutes his brief but glorious
career was ended. It was a
quick summons from that fiery
battle to the spirit world, but
long enough for him to resign
himself to God's forgiving mercy,
through the Lord Jesus Christ,
and to send a loving, comforting
message to his parents. " Tell

my parents that I die happy.
Lord forgive my sins."

"Ah me! that by so frail and feeble
      thread
   Our life is holden; that not life
      alone,
But all that life has won
   May, in an hour, be gathered to the
      dead."

His body was borne tenderly
to the rear by his own men,
whose tears fell on him as they
laid him on the green sward;
and after the retreat, it was recovered, under flag of truce, em-
balmed, and brought for burial
to this house of God, where,
twenty-two years ago, he was

publicly consecrated in the or-
dinance of baptism.

In a letter written at five
o'clock, on the morning of the
preceding day, he has expressed
the feelings with which he entered upon these fatal scenes.
"This, from appearances last
night," he wrote, "is destined to
be *the* day. If we fight, it will
be the hardest of the war, and
it is awful to think of the im-
mense slaughter. I hope I may
be preserved; but if I am not,
I trust only in the merits of a
crucified Saviour, for acceptance
with God." And this last letter
closes with a desire that if he
should be among the dead, his

loss might be tenderly blessed to the dear home he loved so well.

I am permitted to extract from the letter of Captain Best, his commanding officer, a few lines, which reveal the esteem in which his subordinate was held: "Believe me, when I say that this shock is nearly as great a one to me as it can be to you. Lieutenant Crosby was a young man of fine promise, unexceptionable in his habits and moral character; a Christian who practised what he believed; ambitious in his profession, and willing to stand by the government in all its measures. He had my

company in splendid condition,
and fought it well."

To these statements of his
military career one thing should
be added. His connection with
these scenes of war was only
for a purpose and for a time.
When I last spoke with him,
standing there close by the spot
where his coffin is now placed,
I asked him: "Are you in for
this service permanently, or only
till the war is over?" His re-
ply was: "I shall be very glad
to be back in the old place, but
I must do my duty to the end."
His was no craving for military
position and renown, but a pure,
patriotic fervor which made him

a soldier from principle, so long as his country needed his sword; that service finished, he longed to take his place again in peace-ful scenes, and live apart from strife and war.

This record should not close without a further reference to the consistency of his Christian character, amid the trying scenes of his career. We can all real-ize how great a trial of the faith of a young Christian it must be to stand up for Jesus amid the corruptions of the camp, and in the carnage of the battle. Our dear friend never forgot that he was Christ's soldier before he was the soldier of the nation.

His letters show a real growth
in grace and Christian manhood
during his military life. In one
he writes: "Another Sabbath is
just past, one in which I have
very much felt the want of some
Christian friend to converse with.
I am, as it were, alone, but not
alone, for there is one Friend
who always is with those who
trust in him. I pray that I
may be enabled to live nearer
to him, to put more implicit
trust and confidence in his
doings, to have more faith in
his word, and to do more for
his cause than I have ever done.
At times I feel very despondent,
for I do not seem to have made

any progress in the Christian
life, but to be continually more
and more falling short of my
duty. I lack perseverance. Oh!
that Christ might strengthen me
to do his work!'

That these were really the
aspirations of a soul hungering
and thirsting after righteousness,
is evident, as one traces the
manner of his daily life. I find
him laboring for the spiritual
welfare of his men, talking about
Christ to his negro servant, acting as chaplain at the burial
of his soldiers; on one occasion
reading the eleventh chapter of
St. John's gospel, making com-
ments upon it, and offering pray-

er.   He was kind to the sick,
patient with the erring, atten-
tive to every little duty, winning
thus the entire devotion of his
command.   I have read the testimony of an unbeliever and
skeptic concerning him.   " He
was a true Christian."

Many of his letters are radiant
with his Christian experience.
"What a glorious, blessed thing,"
he writes, "is the Christian religion !   How simple and how
wonderful !   I have, this past
week, been enabled to live much
nearer to Christ than ever before.   And while I have enjoy-
ed it much, it makes me desire, more strongly than ever,

to live wholly to him. The whole religion is summed up in the one word 'faith,' and that mine might be increased is my earnest prayer. And when this faith is perfected in sight, what a blessed experience will be ours! At times I feel as if I could almost wish for trouble and suffering, to bring me near to Christ. How happy we shall be when we all meet around the throne of God in heaven, where is no more sin or sorrow, and where we shall know Christ as we ought! That through his righteousness all our dear relations may have this blessing, is my prayer."

I look with admiration upon this fair example of a Christian character, coupled with so much devotion to the stern, rugged war-work to which he was appointed. So brave, and yet so gentle; so thoughtful for others; so unsparing of himself; so pure in his morality, and yet so reliant on his Saviour's righteousness. I utter only the honest convictions of my heart in saying, that while among the heroes who have fallen in this strife, he may take rank with Greble, with Ellsworth, and with Winthrop, his name and memory are also worthy of a place, in Christian annals, by the side

of those of Major Vandeleur
and Headley Vicars, of the Brit-
ish army, or Frazer Stearns,
and Chaplain Butler, of our own.

> "Soldier of Christ, well done ;
>   Rest from thy stern employ:
> The battle fought, the victory won,
>   Enter thy Master's joy.

> "The voice at day-dawn came ;
>   He started up to hear ;
> The mortal bullet pierced his frame,
>   He fell—but felt no fear.

> "Soldier of Christ, well done ;
>   Praise be thy new employ ;
> And while eternal ages run,
>   Rest in thy Saviour's joy."

To the young men who were
his comrades and companions we
commend this radiant picture

of a heroic Christian life. His course is finished; but although dead, he still is speaking to us. The lesson of his sacrifice bids us cherish those two great objects of devotion which he loved so well — that *flag*, our country's emblem, which now enfolds him with its stars and stripes; that *cross* to which on earth he came, and before whose ascended Sufferer he now stands, clothed in a beauty not of earth.

ADDRESS

BY

REV GEO. L. PRENTISS, D.D.

———•♦•———

As I look over this great congregation, my mind's eye reverts to another assembly convened in this same sanctuary some nine years ago. How well I remember the impressive scene which presented itself, as standing in this place I ministered at the altar of God, on that Sabbath afternoon in the pleasant month of October! How vividly I recall from among the faces that then shone upon me that of the sainted grandfather* of him whose mortal remains lie before us. Who that saw him will ever forget that eye or that face? He was one of the best men I ever knew. I esteem it one of the privileges of my life to have been his pastor and friend, and I esteem it a privilege hardly less to have been so long the pastor and friend of the noble youth whose early confession of Christ he watched that afternoon with such tender interest, and around whose bier we are gathered this morning.

* The late Hon. Benjamin F. Butler.

It would be wrong, my friends,
to say that we have not been
summoned to this house of God
on a mournful errand. A great
private and public loss has called us together. The sudden ex-
tinction of so much manly
strength and beauty, of so much
Christian promise, must needs
excite emotions of sharp regret
in every bosom.

To weep with those that weep
is a sacred duty; and who of
us does not feel like doing so
now? For myself I would
gladly leave this pulpit, take
my place among the mourners,
and mingle my tears with theirs.
Certainly they need our warm-

est sympathies. Oh! how many bright hopes, what ardent and dear affections, what a fair promise of useful and happy days, lie buried in this coffin! And yet, blessed be God! there is another side to the picture, a side radiant with immortal joy and peace. He whom we mourn has indeed been snatched from us in the very prime of manhood; but, as you have just heard, with what fine Christian qualities was that early manhood adorned! The days of two and twenty summers sufficed to ripen in him the loveliest virtues. He had the innocence, the joyousness, and the simple tastes of a pure-minded, happy boy, combined with the intelligent vigor, the loyalty, courage, and determination of maturest years. But the most striking feature of his character, as I recall him, was that to which allusion has already been made — his ardent, filial piety. Nothing could be more charming than this trait, as it appeared in the domestic circle, of which he was such a "bright, particular star." All who knew him in the bosom of his family will bear witness to his rare devotion, both as a son and brother. The first words which he is reported to have uttered, after

the fatal bullet pierced his side,
"*Tell my parents that I die happy*,"
are as characteristic as they are
touching and beautiful. Nature
and grace conspired to render,
him dear to his friends. It
would take a long time to give
full utterance to my own affection for him, and my high es-
timate of his worth. But, while
I shall attempt no labored eulo-
gy, there are some features of
his Christian character which
seem to me deserving of special
emphasis. You have just been
told that he chose the profession
of arms, not because he desired
it, but from an overwhelming
sense of duty. I well remember

his decision to go into the army.
It so chanced that I was spend-
ing a few weeks under his father's roof at the time. I had
several conversations with him
on the subject, and am quite
sure that he consecrated himself
to the service of his imperiled
country with a self-devotion not
less pure and entire than that
with which, nine years ago, he
here offered himself to God, and
took the sacramental oath of
allegiance to Jesus Christ. His
piety was the very soul of his
patriotism.

I hold in my hand a little
book, whose name is familiar
as a household word through-

out Christendom. It is a book
marked by some faults, but full
of holy thought and pious coun-
sels. For several centuries it
has been a manual of the Christian life to many myriads of
saints. It is *The Imitation of
Jesus Christ.* I find that our
young friend took with him this
little book, upon setting out for
the war. It passed into his
hands in August, 1861, and
passed out of them only with
his life. That he read it often
and carefully is evident from the
number of passages which bear
his pencil-marks. And here let
me say, that such marks on the
books he reads afford an almost

infallible test of a man's moral
and religious taste.   There are
old family Bibles which contain,
in simple lines on the margin,
the history of many a devout
and eminently useful life.   How
often has the life of the devoted
minister or missionary of the
cross been written in these dumb
characters upon the pages of
God's Word!   Now the passages
marked in this little book are
very   striking   in   one   respect ;
they nearly all indicate a severe
inward conflict such as no one
would   have   anticipated   in   a
young man so full of life and
spirits.   You will perceive the
nature of the conflict if I read to

you a few sentences. In the table
of contents I find these two chap-
ters specially marked : " How a
desolate person ought to offer
himself into the hands of God."
" We ought to offer up ourselves
and all that is ours unto God."
And, in the body of the work,
of the many passages marked,
allow me to read a few: " Fight
like a good soldier ; and if thou
sometimes fall through frailty,
take again greater strength than
before, trusting in my more abun-
dant grace." " Christ's whole life
was a cross and martyrdom, and
dost thou seek rest and joy for
thyself?" "Sometimes thou shalt
be forsaken of God, sometimes.

thou shalt be troubled by thy
neighbor; and, what is more,
oftentimes thou shalt be weari-
some to thyself; neither canst
thou be delivered or eased, by
any remedy or comfort, but so
long as it pleaseth God thou
oughtest to bear it." " Be mind-
ful of the profession thou hast
made, and have always before
the eyes of thy soul the re-
membrance of thy Saviour crucified."

I will read but a single pas-
sage more : " There is scarcely
any thing wherein thou hast
such need to die to thyself as
in seeing and suffering those
things that are adverse to thy

will, especially when that is commanded to be done which seemeth unto thee inconvenient or useless."

It is not likely that such a book should have been taken to the camp, and there read so often, and that many such passages should have been marked by one whose spiritual life was not in vigorous exercise. It is plain, that while fighting in the service of his country, this gallant young soldier was also fighting earnestly the good fight of faith, and laying hold on eternal life.

This occasion, then, is one of joy as well as sadness; nor can

I close without congratulating you, my dear brother, and all this bereaved family circle, upon the rare privilege of having possessed such a son, such a young relative and friend, for the service of Christ and of our afflicted country. I look upon this lamented youth as a type of the young American patriot and Christian soldier; and I do not doubt that out of this war, out of all these public and private tribulations, there will come forth a great company, fashioned after the same pattern. We shall have thousands and tens of thousands of them. Let the old men who hear me, and whose hearts sink within them at 'the sight of so many of our noblest youth cut down in their beauty, comfort themselves with this thought. The blood of these young soldiers of the republic is to be the seed of a better church and state of the future. A new race of American citizens will arise, who shall live, and move, and have their being, first in God, and then in the service of this vast and glorious commonwealth of Christian order, freedom, and humanity, which we have inherited from our fathers. I say, therefore, that even in the presence of this great bereavement, we have am-

ple reason for joy and thanksgiving. We can not but praise
God as we look back over the
beautiful life so early sacrificed
upon the altar of our country;
nor can we help rejoicing as we
look forward and see thousands
taking lessons of patriotic devotion from the example, and
eagerly treading in the footsteps
of this heroic youth. Let not
our souls be cast down nor dis-
quieted within us. Let us hope
still in God, and commit our
imperiled Union, with all the
vast interests at stake, into His
omnipotent hands, assured beyond a doubt that, as He led
our fathers like a flock, so He

will lead us, and, in due time,
bring the whole nation forth,
out of this sea of trouble, with
the voice of praise and thanksgiving upon its lips; and when
we are gone, He will take our
children and our children's children by the hand, and guide them
also in the right way, even to
the latest generation. In this
cheering faith let us return to
the work of life, and press forward with unfaltering steps, until we pass into "a better country, that is, a heavenly," and
there join our departed Christian
friends, and the saints of all
ages, in ascribing blessing, and
honor, and glory, and power,

unto Him that sitteth upon the throne, and unto the Lamb, for-ever and ever. Amen.

RESOLUTIONS.

AT a meeting of the Class of 1860, New-York Free Academy, held May 13th, 1863, the following resolutions were unanimously adopted :

Whereas, By the death of Lieutenant Franklin B. Crosby, of the Fourth United States Artillery, killed at the battle of Chancellorsville, on the third day of May, 1863, we lost another classmate; and

Whereas, We deem it our duty to honor manliness and Christian virtue, and to bear our testimony to their existence ; therefore, be it

Resolved, That in Franklin B. Crosby we lost a classmate who, as a scholar, reflected honor on us in the past, and would have continued so to do by his ability, his learning, and the success he was certain to attain in that profession from the study of which he was called by the demands of a patriotism to which his life was a sacrifice; a friend, warm, trusted, and beloved; a man who, carrying his Christian principles without pretension, into all the relations of life, was modest, energetic, and true. And

Resolved, That in his answer, given shortly before his death, at the post of duty, " I command it to-day, and intend to command it," we recognize the same modest energy and decision, and the same enduring loyalty to duty, which characterized his whole life, and caused him, at his country's call, to relinquish the luxuries of home, a dear family, many warm friends, and a future of happiness and ease, for the hardships and isolation of the camp, and the uncertainties of battle. That in his last words, "I die happy," we have an un-necessary proof of his sincerity, and an assurance that he has "fought the good fight," and gone to reap the rewards of a Christian life. And

Resolved, That we hereby express our sorrow at the loss the community and our country have sustained in the death of so upright and able a man, and so brave and loyal an officer, and we in so dear and honored a classmate and friend. And be it further

Resolved, That we offer his family and friends our sympathies, hoping that, as we are in common deeply grieved at his loss, so in common we may find in his virtues comfort and reconciliation, and objects of emulation.

In Memoriam.

F. B. C.

———

Not so, brave boy, would we have had
    thee die,
If die thou must! On daintiest couch
    to lie,
Soothed with the sweetest ministries of
    love,
Ravished with foretastes of thy home
    above,
Were meet for thee; and on our faith's
    tried wings
To soar from earth and its disquietings.
And when that pure, bright soul had
    sped its way
Joyfully homeward, to the unconscious
    clay

What reverent office had we loved to
    pay !
So would we have it ; but so willed not
    God.
Far from all friends, upon the earth just
    trod
By footsteps dyed in blood, He bade
    thee lie ;
And 'mid the battle's roar Himself alone
    received thy parting sigh.
The "drapery of thy couch" alone en-
    folds thee,
But God in His own sleepless watch yet
    holds thee ;
Thy precious dust is precious in His
    sight ;
Denying it to us, He, day and night,
Himself holds guard. And when His
    morning comes,
We, who lie slumbering in our marble
    tombs,
Shall not spring forth at His arousing
    word

More joyously than he who on the
  sward,
Rather than 'neath it, waits his dearest
  Lord!
Thou, too, O risen Christ! in death
  hast lain!
Thou, too, by wicked, murderous hands
  wast slain!
Oh! help our faltering faith!   Let us be
  still;
And only will what thou, dear Lord,
  dost will ;
Yielding to thee, by choice and not by
  might,
The body and the soul, so precious in
  our sight.
From sunny heights, our loved one, with
  calm brow,
Looks down upon the field where he
  but now
Stood earnest actor. But 'mid heavenly
  joys,

Oh ! what to him are battle's fray and
　　noise ?
His work all done — and in his youth
　　well done —
He early rests with God's eternal Son.
A little while, a few more days of strife,
And we, too, on the battle-field of life,
Shall gaze from those same heights : til.
　　then, O Lord !
Let us toil on, obedient to thy word;
Strong in thy strength, until the vic·
　　tory's won,
And thou shalt say, O faithful souls !
　　well done !　　　　　　　　　　P.

Sunday Evening, May 10, 1863.

The above was written when it was
supposed that the remains of Lieutenant
Crosby could not be recovered.

Franklin Butler Crosby.

Chancellorsville, May 3, 1863.

———

BY WILLIAM ALLEN BUTLER.

———

HE was our noblest, he was our bravest
and best!
Tell me the post that the bravest ever
have filled.
The front of the fight! It was his. For
the rest—
Read the list of the killed.

On the crown of the ridge, where the
sulphurous crest
Of the battle-wave broke, in its thun-
der and flame,
While his country's badge throbbed with
each beat of his breast,
He faced death when it came.

His battery planted in front, the Briga-
 dier cried,
 "Who commands it?" as fiercely the
  foe charged that way;
Then how proudly our gallant Lieutenant replied,
 "I command it to-day!"

There he stood by his guns; stout heart,
 noble form;
 Home and its cherished ones never,
  never so dear,
Round him the whirlwind of battle,
 through the wild storm,
 Duty never so clear.

Duty, the life of his life, his sole guiding
 star,
 The best joy of his being, the smile
  that she gave,
Her call the music by which he marched
 to the war,
 Marched to a soldier's grave.

Too well aimed, with its murderous de
    mon-like hiss,
  To his heart, the swift shot, on its
      errand has flown—
Call it rather the burning, impetuous
    kiss
  With which Fame weds her own !

There he fell on the field, the flag waving
    above,
  Faith blending with joy in his last
      parting breath,
To his Saviour his soul, to his country
    the love
  That was stronger than death.

Ah ! how sadly, without him, we go on
    our way,
  Speaking softer the name that has
      dropped from our prayers ;
But as we tell the tale to our children
    to-day,
  They shall tell it to theirs.

He is our hero, ever immortal and
    young,
With her martyrs his land clasps him
    now to her breast,
And with theirs his loved name shall be
    honored and sung,
Still our bravest and best!

In Memoriam.

Ay! leave the Stripes and Stars
Above him, with the precious cap and
sash;
The mute mementoes of the battle-crash,
And of a hero's scars.

Rest, gallant soldier, rest!
Ennobled e'en in dying: Christ's true
knight
Is now a king, in royal glory bright,
With "Victor" on his crest.

And yet—God giveth sleep;
No earthly victor's laurels ever shed
A glory like the halo round his head.
Ye loved him—should you weep?

Say ye, " His life is lost ;
Our home's sweet comfort, and our crown
of hope" ?
Nay, friends! His life has now a grand-
er scope.
A living holocaust.

To God, and truth, and right,
It aye hath been ; and if the gleaming
coal
On God's own altar hath upborne the
soul
In fiery chariot bright,

'Mid battle roar and strife ;
If to the fearless soldier, God's release
Came swiftly, with the seal of perfect
peace
Upon his earthly life ;

Ay, though it sorely crush
The hearts that clung to him -— poor
hearts that ache

With yearning sense of loss—oh! for his
  sake,
  Each wail of anguish hush!

And yet, ye well may weep,
As those who mourned the holy martyr
  erst,
On whose glad eyes heaven's waiting
  glories burst,
  Before " he fell asleep."

A hero-heart is still,
And eyes are sealed; and loving lips are
  mute,
Which bore on earth the Spirit's golden
  fruit.
  But peace! It was God's will.

And for our precious land—
The land he loved and died for in her
  need,
The blood of heroes is the country's
  seed.
  As he stood, let us stand.

The Lord of hosts doth reign ;
He crowned your soldier, "dying at his
guns."
Oh ! be the nation worthy of such sons—
The noble-hearted slain !

And so we sadly lay,
Yet not all sadly, though with tearful
eyes,
A little nameless flower where he lies,
And gently steal away.